Human Body Systems

# The Respiratory System

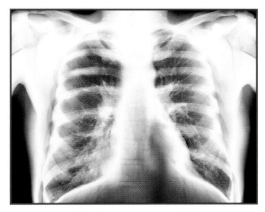

by Rebecca Olien

**Consultant:**
Marjorie Hogan, MD
Pediatrician
Hennepin County Medical Center
Minneapolis, Minnesota

Capstone
press

Mankato, Minnesota

Bridgestone Books are published by Capstone Press,
151 Good Counsel Drive, P.O. Box 669, Mankato, Minnesota 56002.
www.capstonepress.com

*Library of Congress Cataloging-in-Publication Data*
Olien, Rebecca.
    The respiratory system / by Rebecca Olien.
        p. cm.—(Bridgestone books. Human body systems)
    Summary: "Learn about the respiratory system's job, problems that may arise, and how to keep the
system healthy"—Provided by publisher.
    Includes bibliographical references and index.
    ISBN-13: 978-0-7368-5413-9 (hardcover)
    ISBN-10: 0-7368-5413-4 (hardcover)
    1. Respiratory organs—Juvenile literature. I. Title.  II. Series.
QM251.O55 2006
612.2'1—dc22                                                                   2005023803

**Editorial Credits**
Amber Bannerman, editor; Bobbi J. Dey, designer; Kelly Garvin, photo researcher/photo editor

**Photo Credits**
BananaStock, Ltd., 18
Capstone Press/Karon Dubke, cover (girl), 4, 6 (both), 14, 20
Photo Researchers, Inc./Anatomical Travelogue, 8; Bo Veisland, MI&I, 16; Carlyn Iverson, 12;
    Gusto Productions, 1; Science Photo Library/Roger Harris, cover (lungs)
Visuals Unlimited/Ralph Hutchings, 10

# Table of Contents

# Breathing and Blowing

Take a deep breath. Now, blow! You can blow up a balloon because of your respiratory system. This system keeps you alive by breathing the air around you.

The respiratory system is one of several human body systems. These systems all work together to keep your lungs breathing, heart beating, and muscles moving.

◀ Blowing up a balloon takes many deep breaths.

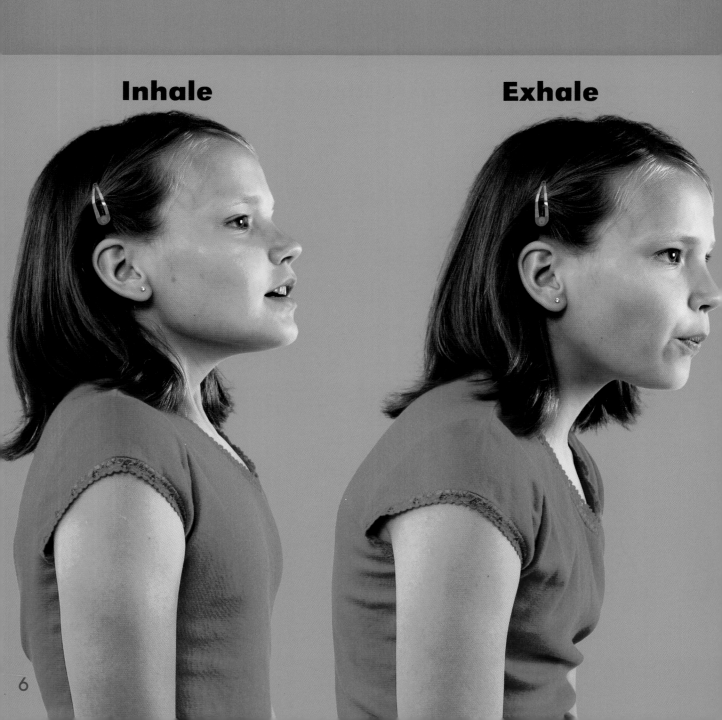

**Inhale**

**Exhale**

# Gases

When you inhale, air carries oxygen into your body. Oxygen is a gas all cells need for energy. Your body needs lots of oxygen. Without it, you could live for only a few minutes.

The respiratory system also gets rid of unwanted gas. Carbon dioxide is a gas that your cells give off as waste. Too much is poisonous to the body. When you exhale, you breathe out carbon dioxide.

◄ Oxygen enters your body when you inhale. Carbon dioxide exits as you exhale.

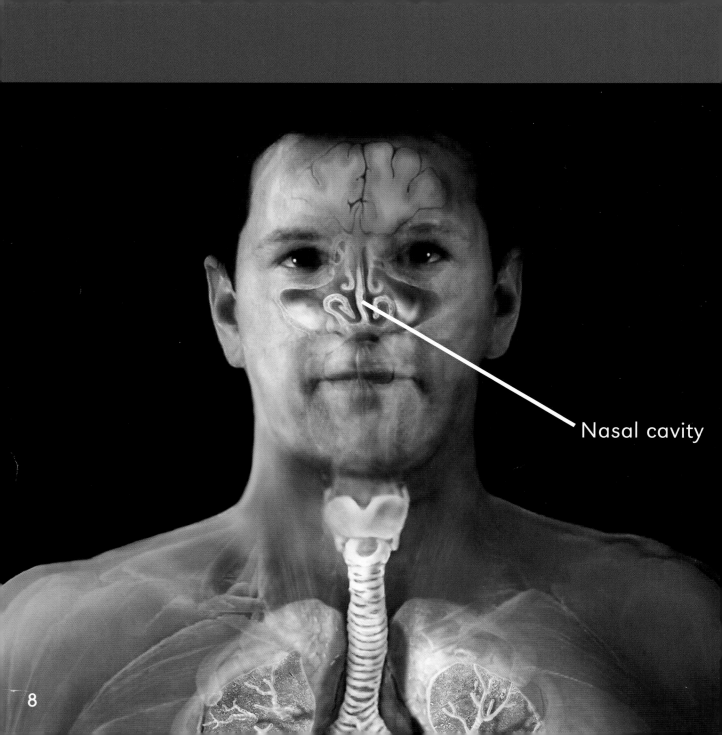

Nasal cavity

# When You Take a Breath

The respiratory system begins with the nose and mouth. When you take a breath, air enters either the nose or mouth. Hairs in the nose trap dirt and other particles.

From your nose, air travels to the nasal cavity. The nasal cavity is like a little cave behind the nose. Air is warmed and moistened there. A thick sticky liquid called **mucus** coats the nasal cavity. Mucus traps germs and dust. Tiny hairs called **cilia** line the nasal cavity and keep mucus moving.

◄ The nose's winding path helps trap germs and dust so they don't travel to the lungs.

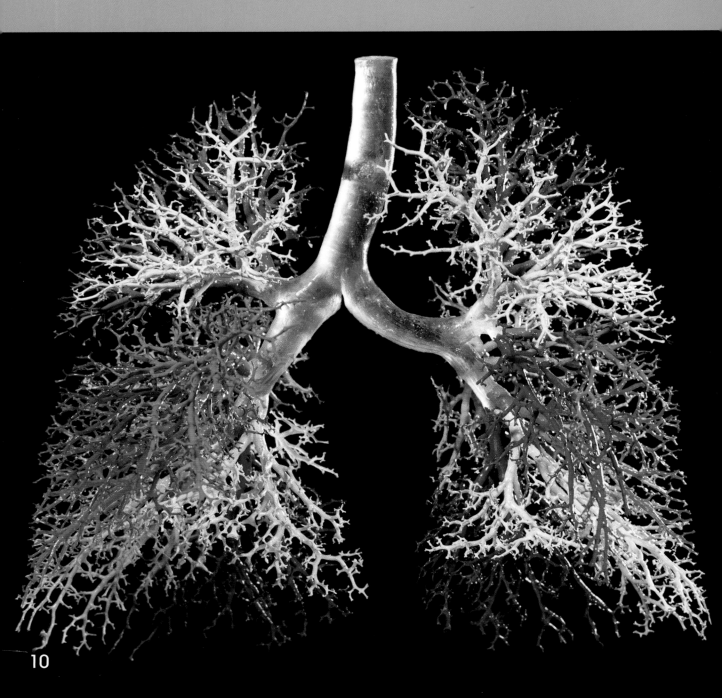

# Getting to the Lungs

From the mouth or nasal cavity, air travels down the throat to the **larynx**. The larynx is often called the voice box. Your larynx holds the vocal cords that you use to speak, scream, and sing.

Next, the air flows through a tube called the **trachea**. The bottom of the trachea splits into two airways. These airways carry air to the lungs.

Air travels through smaller airways in the lungs. At the end of the airways are millions of tiny air sacs called **alveoli**. The alveoli are grouped into clusters like grapes.

◄ A cast of the lungs shows the tiny airways inside.

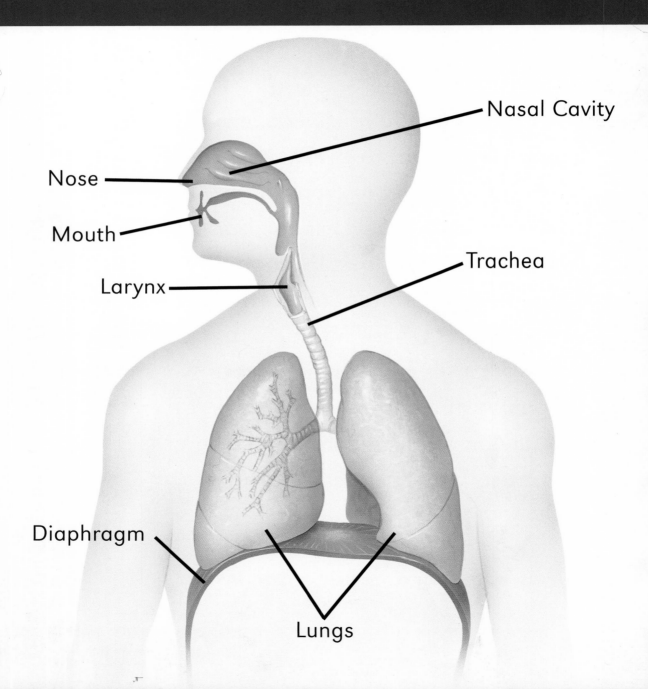

Nasal Cavity

Nose

Mouth

Trachea

Larynx

Diaphragm

Lungs

# Lungs and Diaphragm

Take a deep breath in. Your **diaphragm** muscle pulls your lungs down, while your rib muscles push your chest out. This makes room for your lungs to get bigger. Each lung fills up like a balloon.

Now exhale. Your diaphragm, rib, and chest muscles relax. Air is forced out of your lungs. Each lung shrinks. With each inhale and exhale, your diaphragm, rib, and chest muscles work together to move your lungs.

◀ Your diaphragm helps pull air into your lungs.

# Using Your Voice

The larynx, vocal cords, and mouth help you make sound. Vocal cords stretch across an opening in the larynx. To speak and sing, air is exhaled across the vocal cords. The cords move and make sound waves. The sound waves travel out of your mouth.

Muscles tighten and loosen vocal cords to make different sounds. Tight vocal cords make high-pitched sounds. Loose vocal cords make low-pitched sounds. Mouth and throat muscles help make even more sounds.

◄ Each person has a unique voice.

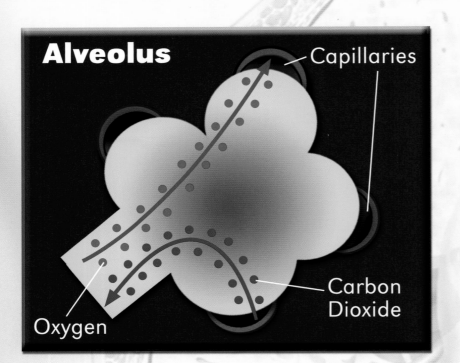

**Alveolus**

Capillaries

Oxygen

Carbon
Dioxide

# Lungs and Heart

The lungs and heart work together to exchange gases at the alveoli. The heart pumps blood through blood vessels. Very small blood vessels called capillaries surround the lung's alveoli. Oxygen travels from the alveoli into the capillaries. Blood carries oxygen to the heart, then throughout the body.

Carbon dioxide is picked up by the blood and carried to the heart. Your heart pumps blood through capillaries to the alveoli. Carbon dioxide leaves your lungs when you breathe out.

◄ Carbon dioxide and oxygen are exchanged in each alveolus of the lungs.

# Respiratory Problems

If you have extra mucus, you probably have a cold. Extra mucus may run down your throat or drip out of your nose. Your body's way of getting rid of extra mucus is by coughing it up or blowing it out.

Extra mucus can also be a sign of **allergies**. People can be allergic to dust, smoke, or mold. Allergies also cause sneezing and watery eyes.

**Asthma** is a lung disease that causes the airways to the lungs to swell and fill with mucus. This makes breathing hard at times. People with asthma usually have allergies too.

◄ Use something to cover your sneeze to prevent germs from spreading.

# Keeping Lungs Healthy

Germs that cause colds are found on things we touch. Washing hands cleans your skin of germs. Keeping hands away from your mouth and nose also stops germs from entering your body.

It's important to keep lungs free of smoke and other pollution. Smoking tobacco is the worst thing you can do to your lungs. Breathing in smoke from other people is also harmful. Staying away from tobacco will help keep you healthy.

◄ Scrub your hands with soap and warm water to get rid of germs.

# Glossary

allergy (AL-lur-gee)—a reaction to something that doesn't cause a reaction in most people; hay fever is an allergy to pollen that makes a person sneeze.

alveoli (al-VEE-uh-lie)—tiny air sacs in the lungs

asthma (AZ-muh)—a lung disease that can make it hard to breathe

cilia (SIL-ee-uh)—short hairs that line the nasal cavity

diaphragm (DIE-uh-fram)—a wall of muscle beneath the lungs; the diaphragm is a muscle used for breathing.

larynx (LA-ringks)—the upper part of the trachea that holds the vocal cords

mucus (MYOO-kuhs)—a slimy liquid coating the inside of the nasal passages and the throat

trachea (TRAY-kee-uh)—the air passage that connects the nose and the mouth to the lungs

# Read More

**Royston, Angela.** *Why Do I Sneeze?: And Other Questions About Breathing.* Heinemann Infosearch. Chicago: Heinemann, 2003.

**Ylvisaker, Anne.** *Your Lungs.* The Bridgestone Science Library. Mankato, Minn.: Bridgestone Books, 2002.

# Internet Sites

FactHound offers a safe, fun way to find Internet sites related to this book. All of the sites on FactHound have been researched by our staff.

Here's how:

1. Visit *www.facthound.com*
2. Type in this special code **0736854134** for age-appropriate sites. Or enter a search word related to this book for a more general search.
3. Click on the **Fetch It** button.

FactHound will fetch the best sites for you!

# Index